The Last Battlefield Monument in America? Book
Reviewer Comments

1. "Kudos to you for assembling for publication this outstanding documentation of the creation of the Battle of Bladensburg Monument…In my admittedly biased judgment, the photographs and your narrative documenting the complex process are exceptional."

         - Dick Charlton – Founding Board Member, retired Treasurer, and Chairman – Aman Memorial Trust

2. "The thought did occur to me, related to the importance of our book as a record, about how critical this could be to a future researcher…I don't think you have to make any changes – it looks good to me."

         - Edward Day, Chief Historic Preservation Officer – Maryland-National Capital Parks and Planning Commission

3. "Great job…the book is terrific…I liked the night photos…"

         - John Giannetti, Sr., Founding Board Member and retired Chairman – Aman Memorial Trust

4. "Hi John, good to hear from you and my compliments on a spectacular battle monument."

         - Jim Lighthizer – President Emeritus – American Battlefield Trust

5. "Great job. I enjoyed the read."

         - Sam Parker – Board Member, Maryland Historical Trust, and former Maryland National Capital Park and Planning Commission Chairman

The Last Battlefield Monument in America?

John Sower

Board Member, Aman Memorial Trust

Founder, Friends of the Battle of Bladensburg

The Last Battlefield Monument in America?

Copyrights © 2024 by John Sower

All Rights Reserved

No part of this book may be reproduced or transmitted in any form or by any means, electronic or mechanical, including photocopying, recording, or by any information storage and retrieval system without the written permission of the author, except where permitted by law.

This book is dedicated to John Giannetti, Sr., Chairman and Dick Charlton, Treasurer of the Aman Memorial Trust and to the government officials and private citizens who assisted in building the Battle of Bladensburg Monument.

Thanks to John Giannetti, Sr., Dick Charlton, Sam Parker, Susan Pearl, Kathleen Sower, and Michele LaPrell for editing assistance.

Table of Contents

Preface i

Chapter One: Introduction and Summary 1

Chapter Two: The Sculpture 6

Chapter Three: The Limestone Base 15

Chapter Four: The Granite Interpretive Panels 19

Chapter Five: The Monument Site 33

Chapter Six: The Funding 35

Chapter Seven: The Team 39

Chapter Eight: The Partners 42

Chapter Nine: The Governor's Award 48

Postscript: Personal Notes 50

About the Author 52

Preface

The pending 10th anniversary of the Dedication of the War of 1812 Battle of Bladensburg Monument on August 24, 2014, was the incentive to organize these files and photos.

This book contains several stories:

- The planning, funding, and construction of the Monument.
- The team of volunteers who were responsible.

It is dedicated to:

- John Giannetti, Sr., Chairman, and Dick Charlton, Treasurer, of the Aman Trust
- The government officials and private citizens who helped.

Battlefield monuments usually start "top-down" with official government-appointed commissions with designated funding.

The War of 1812 Battle of Bladensburg Monument was built "bottom-up" by volunteers with no official sanction and little initial funding.

When people ask about the Battle of Bladensburg Monument, this book will tell its story.

Chapter One: Introduction and Summary

Crisis

"The truck has broken down in Indiana. I don't know how long we'll be delayed."

The truck driver transporting granite interpretive panels for the War of 1812 Battle of Bladensburg Monument from a stone quarry in Northern Minnesota sent this message.

The Aman Memorial Trust, a volunteer group, had been working for four years to build a Monument commemorating the War of 1812 Battle of Bladensburg, and they were nearly finished.

The call came late on Friday night, August 15, 2014, only a week before the 200th anniversary Dedication ceremony of the Battle on August 24, 2014.

On the truck were three large granite panels with colored inserts and narrative wording that told the story of the Battle of Bladensburg. The truck was stranded on the Indiana Turnpike at night and might not arrive in time.

The volunteer group had previous delays and crises in building the Monument:

- In 2011, with three years to go, the group learned that the State of Maryland had declined their first grant request for funds to build the Monument.
- In 2012, with two years to go, the group learned that local officials objected to the number of words on the granite panels and delayed the funding.
- In 2012, the group also learned that the State of Maryland had reduced a second grant request by allocating part of the funds to build a visitor center.
- In 2013, they learned that the large limestone blocks at the base of the Monument had been cut incorrectly.
- Lastly, only a week before the long-awaited Dedication, there was news that the truck broke down in Indiana.

After many tense moments, the group resolved these crises. The State of Maryland finally approved the grant requests. The wording on the granite panels was accepted. The stone contractor replaced the limestone blocks. Local officials identified a visitor center site.

The truck finally arrived, and the granite panels were installed days before the Dedication.

The Battle of Bladensburg

The Battle of Bladensburg occurred in August 1814. British forces defeated the American troops fighting to prevent the British from reaching the nation's capital. The British soldiers then invaded Washington, DC, and burned the Capitol Building, the White House, and other buildings.

Unlike most Revolutionary and Civil War battlefields, the Battle of Bladensburg site was not preserved, and it is now built over with houses, stores, and even a cemetery.

Before the Battle of Bladensburg Monument, no memorials or historical markers on public property commemorated the battlefield or told the story of the Battle.

Sadly, Americans had fought and died there defending their country, but that chapter of American history was ignored and forgotten.

Aman Memorial Trust

The vision to build a Monument commemorating the Battle of Bladensburg came from John Giannetti, Sr, a local businessman, artist, former Marine Captain, and history enthusiast.

John was chairman of the Aman Memorial Trust, a small foundation established to promote the preservation and maintenance of historic buildings and monuments in the Bladensburg area. John Giannetti, Sr, Dick Charlton, Charles Day, and Sam Parker, who were local businessmen, history enthusiasts, and preservationists, were on the Board.

John recruited Joanna Blake, a nearby resident and sculptor who had worked on the World War II Memorial in Washington, DC. They visited monuments in Baltimore for ideas for a Battle of Bladensburg Monument. The Aman Trust had sufficient funds to contract with Joanna in August 2011 and got her started.

Town of Bladensburg

The Town of Bladensburg is a small, multi-ethnic, moderate-income community located on a tributary of the Potomac River near Washington, DC.

In 2010, Bladensburg's then-Mayor Walter James organized a War of 1812 Battle of Bladensburg Task Force to plan for the 200th anniversary of the Battle of Bladensburg. This group organized anniversary events and discussed sites for a visitor center.

The Monument

The Battle of Bladensburg Monument is in Bladensburg, where the British forces gathered to cross the Anacostia River bridge and attack the defending Americans.

The Monument has three parts:

- A bronze sculpture depicting the action on the battlefield
- Three large granite panels with color images and a narrative explaining the battle
- A limestone base

The site for the Monument is near the World War I Peace Cross Memorial and monuments commemorating other events.

Dedication

The Dedication of the Monument was held on the 200th anniversary of the Battle of Bladensburg on August 23, 2014. Speakers included Maryland Governor Martin O'Malley and Maryland State Senate President Mike Miller. Both were history enthusiasts and supporters of the Monument. Other speakers included John Giannetti, Sr. and Joanna Blake.

Conclusion

Those who participated in planning and building the Monument are very proud.

It is a unique battlefield monument because:

1. It has a narrative that, after 200 years, tells the story of the Battle.
2. It has color images depicting the Battle and those involved.

There are no other known battlefield monuments with these two features.

The first battlefield monument on American soil, built in 1799, commemorates the Battle of Lexington (Massachusetts), which started the American Revolutionary War.

The last battlefield monument on American soil (to date), built in 2014, commemorates the Battle of Bladensburg.

These two monuments are the "bookends" of American battlefield monuments, with many battlefield monuments between them.

Photos

1-1: Cover page

1-2: Sculpture at night

1-3: Granite panels at night.

1-2

1-3

Chapter Two: The Sculpture

Introduction

The most visible feature of the Monument is the bronze relief sculpture by Joanna Blake. She was a local resident who had worked on the World War II Monument on the National Mall in Washington, DC. She was recommended to John Giannetti, Sr. by Raymond Kaskey, a sculptor and architect of large civic art pieces – including parts of the World War II Monument in DC.

Titled "Undaunted in Battle," the sculpture depicts Commodore Joshua Barney, an American hero of the battle, after he was shot in the right leg. He is supported by Charles Ball, a former slave who was a member of Barney's Navy Flotilla and a Marine. All three figures are facing forward, "undaunted."

John Giannetti, Sr. said: "We wanted to show that even though the battle was lost, some of the militia and the marines refused to retreat and tried to stop the British. Many of them were killed, and some were wounded. These guys deserved recognition." (Gazette 12-27-13) "I'd compare it to the Alamo, " he said. "They put their life on the line and fought without fear, and this monument is a tribute of gratitude." (Gazette 8-22-14)

On April 14, 2010, Joanna described how she and John got started with the Monument: "John Giannetti approached me a few months ago about the Aman Trust's interest in creating a sculpture to commemorate the Battle of Bladensburg. In March, John and I visited Baltimore to see several War of 1812 monuments. Most combine stone and bronze, the most fitting materials for lasting outdoor sculpture. While they varied in size, the artworks seemed to have a similar feel; they conveyed a sense of triumph. It was clear then that the challenge for a memorial in Bladensburg was to convey a defeat in a single Battle, in which the War was ultimately won."

"The figures will be sculpted in relief and cast in bronze. The bronze panel will be on a limestone base that reads "Undaunted in Battle" below the sculpture. The base of the memorial is low, unlike the towering triumphant monuments in Baltimore, with a shape that more closely resembles that of a mausoleum. The "back" of the base, opposite the sculpture, could be carved with inscriptions about historical events. The site we are proposing is the Bladensburg Balloon Gardens. Its central location and the fact that the battle occurred nearby make it an ideal spot. With the sculpture and surrounding landscape, we hope to create a space for reflection, a destination for tourists interested in history, and a reminder to the residents of Port Towns of the historical significance of the events that took place in their hometown."

The Process

It was interesting to watch Joanna prepare the sculpture. She drew concept drawings and sketches, hired human models, made a quarter-scale model, sculpted a full-size model, and then made a mold that she sent to Laran Bronze in Chester, PA, to make the actual bronze sculpture.

The initial agreement between Aman Trust and Joanna was dated August 26, 2011, for $17,000. Aman and Joanna signed contract amendments as the sculpture progressed, and the total cost ended at $50,000. Aman signed the contract with Laran Bronze in January 2013 for $62,260.

Laran Bronze delivered the completed bronze to Bladensburg on a trailer and mounted it on the Monument's limestone base. As the large bronze sculpture was hanging in straps from a crane and moving slowly through the air to the limestone base, someone asked Ray Kaskey how often these sculptures fit correctly on the first try. His discouraging response was "about 50% of the time". Fortunately, Joanna had done her job, and the sculpture fit perfectly. There was a loud round of cheers from the workers and attendees.

The sculpture is large, approximately 10 ft wide and 8 ft high.

The Figures on the Sculpture

Joshua Barney is a little-known American hero. He was an American Naval officer during the Revolutionary War and later served in the French Navy. During the War of 1812, he led the Chesapeake Bay Flotilla, a fleet of small gunboats defending Chesapeake Bay. When the British Navy moved up the Patuxent River toward Washington, DC, Barney took most of his men and participated in the Battle of Bladensburg, trying to defend Washington. He led the resistance to invading British soldiers and was wounded in battle. However, their efforts were not successful, and the British advanced into Washington, DC, and burned the US Capitol, the White House, and other buildings before retreating.

Charles Ball, a tragic figure, was a former slave who had escaped from the South and served for a year in the Navy with Commodore Barney. After the War of 1812, he was captured and returned to slavery in the South. While en route, he went through Bladensberg, where he saw the battlefield and later wrote ironically and sadly, "… I fought in the ranks of the army of the United States, in defense of the liberty and independence of that which I regarded as my country." He escaped slavery in the South, moved to Pennsylvania, wrote a memoir, and then disappeared. He could not reunite with his family because they were captured and sent South.

The third person in the sculpture, a Marine, isn't named, although a group of Marines fought with Barney in Bladensburg. John Giannetti, Sr. joined the Marines in 1962 and became an officer. Despite the many problems and delays in building the Monument, he always displayed the Marine spirit of not giving up.

The Sculptor

Tragically, Joanna Blake was killed in a motorcycle accident at age 39 on May 22, 2016, while on vacation in Italy. WUSA9 reported how her friends were mourning the loss of a "rising star." (May 25, 2016)

The year before, on August 24, 2015, at the first-anniversary dinner of the Monument, Joanna was toasted: "In addition to being talented and intelligent, she knows her craft and is very hard-working. She was cerebral and able to understand abstract concepts like patriotism, racial sensitivities, and liberty - and translate them into the reality of bronze".

Photos

2-1a, 2-1b, 2-1c: Three concept drawings of the sculpture

2-2: Joanna Blake and John Giannetti, Sr. with the partially completed full-scale model

2-3: (L to R) Charles Day, John Giannetti, Sr., Susan Pearl, Sam Parker, and Dick Charlton with the completed full-scale model

2-4: The sculpture being installed

2-5: The sculpture being installed

2-6 The sculpture being installed

2-7 The sculpture being installed

2-8: Close-up of the final sculpture,

2-9: Close-up of the final sculpture.

2-1a

2-1b

2-1c

2-2

2-3

2-4

2-6

2-5

2-7

2-8

2-9

Chapter Three: The Limestone Base

The first step in building the monument was preparing plans and specifications. Based on the preliminary concept sketches prepared by Joanna Blake and John Giannetti Sr. on July 19, 2011, Aman Trust contracted with Corinthian Stoneworks and Design to prepare them.

Next, on September 26, 2011, Aman Trust sent a Design-Build RFP (Request for Proposal) to five local stone contractors. They all responded, and the Pagliaro Brothers Stone Co. proposal was selected based on price, professional credentials, and design suggestions. After negotiations, the total cost for constructing the limestone base was agreed to be $180,000.

The limestone blocks are on a concrete foundation; the largest are 61" wide, 29" thick, and 48" high, making the monument nearly 16 ft tall and 3 ft wide at the bottom.

A crisis occurred when the large limestone blocks arrived. The Aman Trust realized they were cut incorrectly and could not hold the bronze sculpture. There was a disagreement about whether the contractor mismeasured or whether Aman Trust had inadvertently approved incorrect drawings. It was resolved by splitting the $15,000 additional cost with the contractor and replacing the limestone blocks.

Other steps needed for starting on the limestone base included:

- o Getting M-NCPPC's approval of the design plan.
- o Getting Prince George's County approval of the construction permits.
- o Doing soil borings to determine the needed depth of the concrete foundation.

Photos

3-1: Start of construction with John Giarmetti, Sr., John Sower, and Dick Charlton.

3-2: Start of construction- group photo.

3-3: Pouring concrete.

3-4: Installation of reinforcement bars.

3-5: Construction of wood frame.

3-6: Completed construction.

3-1

3-2

3-3

3-4

3-5

3-6

Chapter Four: The Granite Interpretive Panels

The third part of the monument was large granite panels with wording and pictures telling the story of the Battle of Bladensburg.

The Wording Crisis

The quantity of wording on the panels was controversial and caused a year's delay. John Giannetti Sr.'s company, Giannetti's Studio, was in Brentwood, MD, near the Monument site. Daily, he drove through the Battlefield site when commuting from his home. He lamented as a Marine officer that there were no monuments or other indications of the battle there - where Americans had fought a foreign invading army and lost their lives defending their nation's capital. One of his goals in building a Monument was to "tell the story" of the Battle of Bladensburg.

The three black granite panels are each 3 ft wide and almost 9 ft high. The print is colored a soft gray -like the wording on the Korean War monument on the Washington Mall.

On the central bronze panel are color images of the U.S. and British flags, the wording "Undaunted* Battle of Bladensburg * 1814", a historic print entitled "Last Stand at Bladensburg," a historical map of the battlefield site, images of Commodore Joshua Barney, US Navy Flotilla Commander, who led the American forces, and of Major General Robert Ross, the British Army Commander.

Also on the center panel in large print are the words:

>"This Monument stands as
>A tribute to the American
>Soldiers, Sailors, and
>Marines who fought and
>Died here defending their
>Nation's Capital."

Then it has color pictures of Barney and Ross, followed by two sentences:

"The Monument depicts Commodore
Joshua Barney of the U.S. Navy, a moment after being wounded by the
approaching British troops. Barney
is assisted by Charles Ball, a former slave,
and flotillaman of the U.S.
Navy, and by a U.S. Marine, part of
a force of nearly 500 troops who
refused to retreat until ordered to
by their commander and stood
"Undaunted in Battle" in defense
of Washington, D.C."

On the left and right panels, the wording describes the Battle of Bladensburg:

"On August 19, 1814, approximately 4500 British troops under the command of Major General Robert Ross landed in Southern Maryland and marched to Upper Marlboro. The British convened a council of war and marched toward Washington, intent on attacking the capital. They arrived in Bladensburg on August 24, 1814.

The American force, numbering nearly 6,000 and composed mainly of militia units with U.S. Army, Navy, and Marine regulars, occupied the ground across the river from Bladensburg. The British troops, who arrived at noon, crossed the bridge and engaged the American forces on the far bank. The British fired Congreve rockets whose sounds and "red glare" distracted and confused the Americans. The screeching rockets were new but relatively harmless weapons that left billowing smoke trails and caused panic in the ranks of the U.S. troops.

American riflemen and artillery inflicted significant casualties as the British soldiers crossed the bridge. A separate British contingent forded the river to the north and outflanked a militia artillery regiment from Baltimore. U.S. Army General William Winder, commander of the American forces, ordered the troops to fall back, which led to confusion and a full-fledged retreat by the untrained militia.

Although the American forces lost the battle, an epic moment is still remembered with pride - Commodore Barney's final stand. Armed with muskets, boarding pikes, cutlasses, and heavy cannons, Barney's men engaged the British troops with vigor and made several counterattacks. Barney's courageous and undaunted efforts delayed the British and provided valuable time to evacuate the Nation's Capital.

While rallying his troops and directing cannon fire at the British, Barney was severely wounded in his right thigh by a musket ball. Beset on all sides by overwhelming numbers, Barney, unable to stand, ordered his troops to withdraw without him. Barney was captured soon after that.

The victorious British commander, General Ross, recognized the valor and resolute spirit of Commodore Barney and his Marines and flotilla men. He received Commodore Barney's surrender with respect and magnanimity and immediately paroled him.

The British forces marched into Washington, accompanied by Rear Admiral George Cockburn, and torched and burned many government buildings, including the Capitol and White House.

While marching back to their ships, the British arrested Dr. William Beanes of Upper Marlboro. Beanes had angered the British by capturing and jailing British stragglers. Beanes was held on board as a prisoner while the British planned an attack on Baltimore.

Francis Scott Key, a Maryland-born Georgetown attorney, came aboard the British ship, seeking the release of Dr. Beanes. On the night of September 13, 1814, after returning to an American flag of truce ship in Baltimore harbor, Key witnessed the unsuccessful naval bombardment of Fort McHenry and was inspired to pen the "The Star-Spangled Banner" which later became the National Anthem.

Before the bombardment of Fort McHenry, the British had landed at North Point, near Baltimore. During a skirmish there, General Ross, the victor at Bladensburg, was killed in action.

Unable to take Fort McHenry or advance on Baltimore, the British withdrew their forces and eventually left the Chesapeake Bay."

Several local officials insisted that the wording was excessive and should have only the six lines quoted above in the central panel alone, not the more extended narrative about the battle.

They cited the absence of explanatory wording on other monuments, including those at nearby Civil War battlefields. They successfully froze the funding for the granite panels of the monument for a year until State officials resolved the issue.

Aman representatives had several meetings with them to find a compromise but failed. The State officials called several local historians for their opinions to break the stalemate. Fortunately, the first historian they called was Richard Ervin of the Archeological Office of the Maryland Department of Transportation (State Highway Department), who was familiar with the Battle of Bladensburg.

His response was immediate and very supportive of Aman's effort to tell the story. Aman's design for the panels was allowed, and the State grant for the funding was approved.

Wording on America's First Battlefield Monument

Of note is that America's first battlefield monument honored those who fought at the Battle of Lexington, MA, in April 1775. It is in memory of those who fell to the guns of British troops at the start of the American Revolution. It has 31 lines of text explaining the purpose of the monument. Unfortunately, the Aman Trust representatives did not know about the Lexington Monument's wording during the Battle of Bladensburg Monument controversy.

"Sacred to Liberty & the Rights of mankind!!!
The Freedom & Independence of America
Sealed & defended with the blood of her sons

This Monument is erected
By the inhabitants of Lexington,
Under the patronage & at the expense, of
The Commonwealth of Massachusetts,
To the memory of their Fellow Citizens,
Ensign Robert Munroe, Messrs Jonas Parker,
Samuel Hadley, Jonathan Harrington Jun
Issacs Muzzy Caleb Harrington, and John Brown
Of Lexington & Michael Porter of Woburn
Who fell on this field, the first Victims to the
Sword of British Tyranny & Oppression
On the morning of the ever memorable
Nineteenth of April, An. Dom. 1775
The Blood of these Martyrs
In the cause of God & their Country
Was the Cement of the Union of these States, then
Colonies & gave the spring to the spirit Firmness
And resolution of their Fellow Citizens
They rose as one man, to revenge their brethren's
Blood and at the point of the sword to assert &
Defend their native Rights,
They nobly dar'd to be free!!
The contest was long, bloody & affecting
Righteous Heaven approved the solemn appeal,
Victory crowned their arms; and

> The Peace, Liberty & Independence of the United States of America, was their glorious Reward.
>
> Built in the year 1799"

These words still inspire today, especially considering those fighting against tyranny and oppression worldwide.

Maryland State Senate President Mike Miller, a history enthusiast and supporter of the Monument, noted that the Lexington and Bladensburg monuments were like 'bookends' depicting the first and last battlefield monuments built on American soil.

Preparing the Wording

John Giannetti, Sr. and his son John Giannetti, Jr., a lobbyist, former Maryland State Delegate, and Maryland State Senator, wrote the narrative on the Battle of Bladensburg monument.

They wrote multiple drafts and debated the fonts and letter coloring. As shown in the photo, they constructed a life-size model showing how the wording would appear.

Coloring the Images

Putting color in the images on the granite panels was innovative. No other monument in the Washington area is known to have such coloring.

The idea for embedded images was from the Georgetown Waterfront Park in Washington, DC, which has black and white images embedded into granite. Sadly, they have been damaged.

The idea for color images started during a visit to Annapolis, MD. At the U.S. Naval Academy entrance is a large colored map of stone that has faded over the years. Also, the Kunta Kinte – Alex Haley Memorial in the downtown area has vivid colors on white ceramic.

Duane Krueger of Coldspring Granite, a company in Minnesota that was the contractor for the granite panels, said they could embed the color images in a white ceramic material and insert them into the granite panels. They agreed to work with the contractor who had prepared the color images for the Annapolis monument. Aman Trust sent Coldspring the high-resolution color images to embed into the ceramic inserts.

The battlefield image, "Final Stand at Bladensburg," was made in 1985 by Colonel Charles Waterhouse, whose estate permitted using the image in the monument.

The map image, "The Affair of Bladensburg," was from the 1816 atlas in "Memoirs of My Own Times" by General James Wilkinson. The images of Commodore Barney and General Ross are from other historical documents.

The results are dramatic, and the colors remain vivid after ten years. There are no known battlefield monuments with such dramatic coloring- and none that also provide a narrative description of the historical events involved - that 'tell the story.'

Photos

4-1a, 4-1b: Color images of Commodore Barney and Major General Ross.

4-2: The "Undaunted" logo.

4-3a, 4-3b: Battlefield scene and map.

4-4a, 4-4b, 4-4c: Images from Georgetown Waterfront Park, entrance to the U.S. Naval Academy, and the Kunta Kinte - Alex Haley Memorial in Annapolis.

4-5a, 4-5b: John Giannetti, Sr. and John Giannetti, Jr. are planning the granite panels.

4-6: Installing the panels.

4-7: Installing the panels #2.

4-8: Installing the panels #3.

4-9: Installing the panels #4.

4-10a, 4-10b: Lexington Battlefield Monument, Lexington, Mass.

4-11: John Giannetti, Sr. & Dick Charlton and the granite panels.

4-12: Sam Parker and the granite panels.

4-13: Granite Interpretive panels close-up.

4-1a

4-1b

4-2

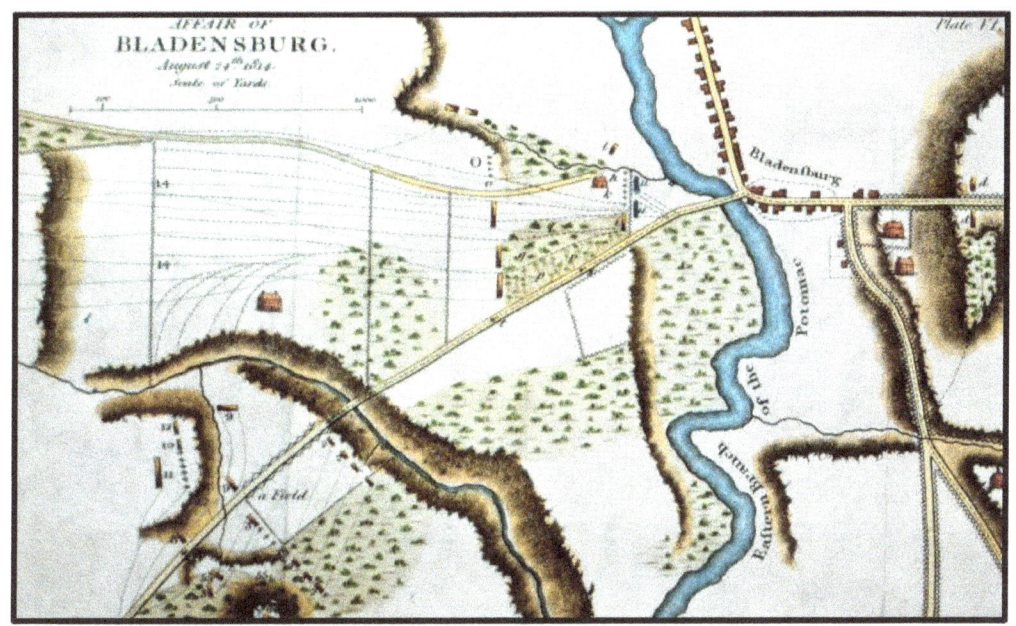

4-3a

4-3b

4-4a

4-4b

4-4c

4-5

4-6

4-7

4-8

4-9

4-10a

4-10b

4-11

4-12

THE BATTLE OF BLADENSBURG
AUGUST 24, 1814

UNDAUNTED
WAR OF 1812

This monument stands as a tribute to the American Soldiers, Sailors, and Marines who fought and died here defending their Nation's Capital.

COMMODORE JOSHUA BARNEY
U.S. NAVY FLOTILLA COMMANDER

MAJOR GENERAL ROBERT ROSS
BRITISH ARMY COMMANDER

The monument depicts Commodore Joshua Barney of the U.S. Navy a moment after being wounded by the approaching British troops. Barney is assisted by Charles Ball, former slave and Flotillaman of the U.S. Navy, and by a U.S. Marine, part of a force of nearly 500 troops who refused to retreat, and stood "Undaunted" in defense of Washington, D.C.

On August 19, 1814, approximately 4500 British troops, under the command of Major General Robert Ross, landed in Southern Maryland, intent on attacking Washington. The British forces marched through Upper Marlboro and arrived in Bladensburg on August 24, 1814.

The American force, numbering nearly 6000, was composed largely of militia units and included U.S. Army, Navy and Marine regulars, occupied the Ground across the river from Bladensburg. The British troops, who arrived at noon, rushed the bridge in force and engaged the Americans on the far bank. The British fired Congreve rockets whose sounds and "red glare" distracted and confused the Americans. The whistling rockets, new but relatively harmless weapons firing blazing red trails, caused panic in the ranks of the U.S. troops.

American sharpshooters and artillery inflicted significant casualties as the British soldiers crossed the bridge. A separate British contingent forded the river to the north and outflanked a militia artillery regiment from Baltimore. U.S. Army General William Winder, commander of the American forces, ordered the troops to pull back, which led to confusion and a full-fledged retreat of the untrained militia.

Although the battle was lost, one epic moment has survived – Commodore Barney's valiant last stand. Armed with muskets, boarding pikes, and cutlasses, Barney's men engaged the British troops with vigor and led several counter-attacks. Barney's courageous and undaunted efforts delayed the British and provided valuable time for the evacuation of the Nation's Capital.

While rallying the troops and directing cannon fire at the British, Barney was severely wounded in his right thigh by a musket ball. Beset on all sides by overwhelming numbers, Barney, unable to stand, ordered his troops to abandon him and withdraw. Barney was captured soon thereafter.

Recognizing the courage, valor, and resolute spirit of the Marines and Flotillamen, the victorious British commander, General Ross, received the surrender of Commodore Barney with the magnanimity and respect due to a brave, wounded foe and immediately paroled him.

Accompanied by Rear Admiral George Cockburn, the British forces marched into Washington, then torched and burned many government buildings, including the Capitol and White House.

While marching back to their ships, the British arrested Dr. William Beanes of Upper Marlboro. Beanes had angered the British by capturing and jailing British stragglers. Beanes was held onboard as a prisoner while the British planned an attack on Baltimore.

Francis Scott Key, a Maryland-born Georgetown attorney, came aboard the same ship, seeking the release of Dr. Beanes. On September 13-14, 1814, while still onboard the British ship in Baltimore harbor, Key witnessed the unsuccessful naval bombardment of Ft. McHenry, and was inspired to pen the "Star Spangled Banner" which later became the National Anthem.

Prior to the bombardment of Ft. McHenry, the British landed at North Point, near Baltimore. During a skirmish, General Ross, the victor at Bladensburg, was killed in action.

Unable to advance on Baltimore, the British then withdrew their forces and eventually left the Chesapeake Bay.

This interpretive panel has been financed in part with State funds from the Maryland War of 1812 Bicentennial Commission.

4-13

Chapter Five: The Monument Site

The monument is located near the World War I Peace Cross and other monuments at the Anacostia River bridge, which the British troops crossed to start the Battle of Bladensburg. Nearby are monuments for World War II, the Korean and Vietnam Wars, the 9-11 attacks, and other events.

The site, formerly Balloon Gardens Park, is across the street from the George Washington House. Aman Trust Board members restored this historic property, an early stagecoach stop between Washington and Baltimore.

The Town of Bladensburg is restoring the nearby Bostwick House, an early 18th-century historic house on an eight-acre tract, with assistance from Aman Trust.

Agreement with M-NCPPC

Although the Maryland National Capital Park and Planning Commission (M-NCPPC) owns the Monument site, Aman Trust proposed to use it for the Bladensburg Monument, and M-NCPPC officials agreed.

Bladensburg

Bladensburg is a small, multi-ethnic, moderate-income community on the Anacostia River near Washington, DC.

Before the American Revolutionary War, Bladensburg was one of only three towns (with Georgetown and Alexandria) in what became the Washington, DC metro area. Merchants in the port traded in tobacco and other products.

Over the years, the Anacostia River flooded, damaging many historic buildings. The river became less navigable, causing a decline in trade. The Army Corps of Engineers eventually controlled the flooding with levees.

Photos

5-1: The George Washington House

5-2: George Washington House historic marker

5-3: Bostwick House

5-4: Peace Cross at night

5-1

5-2

5-3

5-4

Chapter Six: The Funding

The funding for the Bladensburg Monument was complex, with grants from three State of Maryland agencies, funds from M-NCPPC for site improvements, and donations from local community groups, business organizations, and dozens of individuals.

The monument had four parts - each with separate negotiations and funding:

1. The land

2. The limestone base

3. The bronze sculpture

4. The granite panels

The Budget

The Sources and Uses of funds for the monument are summarized below($):

	Bronze Sculpture	Limestone Base	Granite Panels	Total
Uses of Funds				
Sculptor	$ 50,000			50,000
Bronze Foundry	62,260			62,260
Other	7,740			7,740
Subtotal	120,000			120,000
Limestone Base		180,000		180,000
Site Work		50,000		50,000
Subtotal		230,000		230,000
Granite Panels			60,000	60,000
Total	120,000	230,000	60,000	410,000
Sources of Funds				
Aman Trust	85,000	40,000		125,000
Bond Bill	35,000	90,000		125,000
Subtotal	120,000	130,000		250,000
MNCPPC		50,000		50,000
MHAA		50,000		50,000
SS 200			60,000	60,000
Total	$ 120,000	230,000	60,000	410,000

The bronze sculpture cost $120,000, including $50,000 for Joanna Blake, the sculptor, $62,260 for the bronze foundry, and $7,740 for miscellaneous costs. The sources of funds were $85,000 from Aman Trust, and $35,000 from a State of Maryland Bond Bill.

The limestone base cost was $230,000, including $180,000 for the structure and $50,000 for site work. The sources of funds were $40,000 from Aman Trust, $90,000 from the Bond Bill, $50,000 from M-NCPPC, and $50,000 from the Maryland Heritage Areas Authority - a State of Maryland agency.

The Granite Panels cost $60,000, and the source was the Maryland War of 1812 Bicentennial Commission (SS200), which the State of Maryland established to sponsor activities and projects commemorating the 200th anniversary of the War of 1812 in the state.

This budget excludes the Monument site, which was appraised at $446,000 in September 2010, and hundreds of hours of professional volunteers' time by Aman Trust Board members and advisors. If included, the monument's total budget exceeded $1 million.

M-NCPPC

Maryland National Capital Park & Planning Commission (M-NCPPC), which is Prince George's County's park and planning agency, owns the Monument site.

A "Use Agreement" was negotiated wherein M-NCPPC would continue to own the site and invest $30,000 in site improvements and $20,000 for in-kind management time totaling $50,000. Aman Trust could plan and build the monument following plans approved by M-NCPPC.

There were periodic progress meetings with M-NCPPC officials. They participated by cleaning up the site, removing old bushes, leveling the grounds, planting new shrubbery, and installing lighting for the monument at night.

Maryland Bond Bill

The Maryland Department of General Services manages the Maryland Bond Bill program. Aman applied for a Bond Bill grant of $125,000, which included $35,000 for the Bronze Sculpture and $90,000 for the Limestone base.

However, another local group applied for Bond Bill financing for a visitor center (with no specific site or budget identified), and, as a compromise, the approval for the Bond Bill in June of 2011 allocated funds to both projects.

To help resolve this issue, an Aman Trust advisor visited other War of 1812 battlefield visitor centers, including Fort McHenry in Baltimore, the Battle of New Orleans site (Chalmette Battlefield) in New Orleans, and the River Raisin site near Detroit, MI.

He submitted a report comparing those sites and recommending the Bladensburg Waterfront Park site that M-NCPPC owned because it was the right size, had parking, needed no renovation, and because M-NCPPC would pay the costs.

M-NCPPC approved the recommended site, and in January 2013, the state approved Aman's request to use all of the Bond Bill funding ($125,000) for the monument, which provided enough funding to finish construction.

MHAA

The Maryland Heritage Areas Authority (MHAA) provides grants to local communities for community development projects. Grant applications require extensive documentation, including narratives, budgets, photos, renderings, support letters, maps, and resumes.

Aman Trust officials felt the initial application was very competitive because of the plans for the monument, the importance of the Battle of Bladensburg, the absence of any commemoration for 200 years, and the background of the Aman Trust team.

Aman applied to MHAA in March of 2011 and was devastated to receive a denial letter only four months later, in July of 2011. (Aman later learned that Baltimore projects were the initial priority, as there was more time before the 200th anniversary of the Battle of Bladensburg.) Aman re-submitted the MHAA application in 2012, and MHAA approved it in January 2013.

Maryland War of 1812 Bicentennial Commission (SS200)

The State of Maryland had launched a tourism promotion campaign focused on the 200th anniversary of the War of 1812. Fort McHenry is Maryland's leading War of 1812 tourist site, but others are around the state. The SS200 program promoted Maryland tourism internationally and funded dozens of War of 1812 improvement projects around the state.

Aman Trust applied to the SS200 program for $60,000 for the granite panels with narrative and color images telling the story of the Battle of Bladensburg.

Aman applied in October 2011 but did not receive approval until April 11, 2014- only four months before the dedication in August 2014 because of the issue of the amount of narrative on the monument.

Summary

The Battle of Bladensburg Monument was a very broad-based community project that had cooperation and assistance from the State of Maryland officials with the Bond Bill, MHAA, and SS200 agencies, Prince George's County officials from M-NCPPC and the Prince George's County Council, Town of Bladensburg officials, many local community and business groups, and private citizens.

Chapter Seven: The Team

Introduction

Working with the Aman Trust team to plan, finance, and build the Battle of Bladensburg Monument was a unique and rewarding experience.

When they started in 2010, they had:

- Never built a monument
- No management plan
- Very little funding
- No official designation nor authority to build a Monument

They evolved into a team with diverse skills and experience that worked together cooperatively and productively.

Their success was the building of the War of 1812 Battle of Bladensburg Monument.

The Volunteer Team

1. John Giannetti, Sr.: John was the Chairman of the Aman Trust. He lived and worked nearby and wanted to "tell the story" of the Battle of Bladensburg. John was a businessman, a former Marine officer, a history enthusiast, an artist, and a historic preservation activist. He was the co-owner of Giannetti's Studio, Inc., a family-owned business that restored architectural ornamentation in the White House, the Supreme Court Building, and the Library of Congress. He had led the effort to restore the George Washington House. He is a University of Maryland graduate and was a Captain in the US Marine Corps.

2. W. Dickerson (Dick) Charlton: Dick is a retired CPA who was a founder and partner in Millard T. Charlton & Associates, a CPA firm in Bladensburg, for 40 years. They provided accounting services for financial institutions, non-profit organizations, and the healthcare industry. He served as Treasurer of the Aman Memorial Trust for many years. He was responsible for restoring the Magruder House, one of the historic properties in Bladensburg,

and he has been a long-time historic preservation activist. He is Prince George's Representative to the Maryland Historical Trust, and he is a graduate of the University of Maryland

3. Samuel J Parker, Jr.: Sam is an administrator and regional planner who was the former Chairman of the Prince George's County Planning Board and the Maryland-National Capital Park and Planning Commission, the former Chairman of the Board of trustees for Prince George's Community College, and Chairman of the Board of the non-profit Housing Initiative Partnership. Currently, he serves as a Trustee for the Maryland Historical Trust. He is a graduate of the Catholic University of America, has a master's degree in Regional Planning from Cornell University, and is a member of the American Institute of Certified Planners (AICP). Prince George's County Historical Society recently awarded him the St George's Day Award for his activities in historic preservation.

4. John Giannetti, Jr., Esq - John is a lobbyist in Annapolis focused on criminal law, business law, and civil matters. He was a Maryland House of Delegates member from 1999 to 2003, representing Howard and Prince George's Counties, and he was a Maryland State Senator from 2003 to 2007. He graduated from Bucknell University and the University of Maryland School of Law.

5. John Sower - John is the President of Chesapeake Business Finance Corp, a mission lender, making over 300 small business economic development loans in Maryland, DC, and Northern VA, totaling nearly $1 billion. Previously, he assisted with over $2 billion of public and private financing for local economic development projects. He served for ten years on the Board of the International Economic Development Council and for over 40 years on the Board of the National Association of Development Companies. He has a BA in Economics from Lawrence University and an MBA in Finance from the University of Michigan, and he completed the courses for a Ph.D. in Economics from George Washington University. In 2008, he founded Friends of the Battle of Bladensburg.

6. Others on the Aman Trust Board include Charles Day, a retired insurance executive active with many business and community organizations in Prince George's County, and Susan Pearl, a historian on the Prince George's Historical Society Board.

Summary

For four years, from 2010 to August 2014, John Giannetti, Sr., Dick Charlton, and John Sower worked together closely on the Battle of Bladensburg Monument and were in frequent communication. John Giannetti, Sr. and Dick Charlton functioned as the Executive Committee of the Board, and John Sower was the de facto project manager. John Giannetti, Sr., and Dick Charlton made or approved all decisions. There were many frustrations, problems, and delays, but they were resolved.

John and Dick's stature in the community is an essential reason for the project's success. Both had business experience and connections in the Maryland State Capitol in Annapolis. John had construction and contract management experience, and Dick was a CPA with budget and finance experience. John and Dick also had respect and relationships in the community, which enabled them to raise funds from local businessmen and civic organizations.

John Giannetti, Jr. helped as a lawyer and negotiator with Maryland State government officials. Also, his writing expertise and knowledge of printing fonts were valuable.

John Sower's role was writing grant proposals, preparing and maintaining budgets, scheduling progress reports, coordinating schedules, managing grant funding, handling day-to-day operations, and serving as project manager.

Photo

7: (L to R) John Giannetti, Sr., Dick Charlton, John Sower

Chapter Eight: The Partners

Many people and organizations assisted with the monument:

Aman Memorial Trust

The George A. and Carmel D. Aman Memorial Trust was incorporated as a charitable 501 [c][3] organization in November 1983. Its charter states that the purpose was "the preservation and maintenance of historic buildings and monuments in and about the Town of Bladensburg."

John Giannetti, Sr., and Dickerson (Dick) Charlton were incorporating Board members. They stayed active on the Board, along with Charles Day, Susan Pearl, and others, for nearly 40 years, providing leadership and grants for local preservation projects. Samuel J. Parker, Jr., former Chairman of M-NCPPC, joined the Aman Board in the late 1990s.

The Monument is Aman Trust's most prominent project, but the Trust Board members have restored three historic buildings in Bladensburg, including the George Washington House, the Magruder House, and the Market Master's House.

Aman Trust is assisting the Town in restoring Bostwick House, a historic house built in 1746 by a merchant who owned ships, property, and a rope factory and imported and sold slaves.

When the monument was completed in 2014, the Aman Memorial Trust Board included John Giannetti, Sr. (Chairman), Dick Charlton (Treasurer), Charles Day, Susan Pearl, Sam Parker, John Sower, Jim Foster, John Giannetti, Jr., Lee MacLean Doolittle, and Sally Holder.

The 2023 Board included Dick Charlton (Chair), Renee Green (Treasurer), Sam Parker, John Sower, John Giannetti, Jr., Antonette Bruno, Susan Pearl, Steve Weitz, Pam Gilley, Joe Rodriguez, Diane Griffin, and Susan McCutcheon.

Friends of the Battle of Bladensburg

Friends of the Battle of Bladensburg (FOBB) was organized in December 2008 as a non-profit, tax-exempt, charitable 501 [c][3] organization. Its initial board members were John Sower (President and Founder), Michael Schwartz (former President of The Philadelphia Civil War Library & Museum), Wilbur Dove (an expert on non-profit organizations), and John Shick (a retired Naval Captain). FOBB initiated discussions with the Maryland Historical Trust to advocate for historical markers at the site of the Battle of Bladensburg.

John Sower attended local meetings to call attention to the battlefield site and the 200th anniversary of the Battle of Bladensburg. Also, he purchased 2,000 "Friends of the Battle of Bladensburg" blue and white lapel pins, took them to meetings, and distributed them to generate interest in the Battle of Bladensburg.

Friends of the Battle of Bladensburg was de-activated when the organizers became active with Aman Trust on the Monument project.

Mayor's Task Force

Bladensburg Mayor Walter James and Town Clerk Patricia McAuley organized the War of 1812 Battle of Bladensburg Task Force in 2010. It included representatives of local organizations interested in commemorating the 200th anniversary of the Battle.

The Task Force included:

- Pat McAuley, Town of Bladensburg
- Mike Arnold, Prince George's Heritage, Inc.
- Michael Hale, Town of Colmar Manor
- Edward Day, M-NCPPC
- Sandra Kimble, Prince George's County Council District 5
- Richard Cote, Town of Cottage City
- Pat Gladding and Jim Foster, Anacostia Watershed Society
- John Giannetti, Sr. and Dick Charlton, Aman Memorial Trust
- John Sower, Friends of the Battle of Bladensburg
- Cecile Spence, Port Towns CDC
- Aaron Markavitch, Anacostia Trails Heritage Area

- Matthew Neitzey, Prince George's County Conference and Visitors Bureau.

Others later attended meetings and participated.

The Task Force met periodically and considered ideas for programs and projects to commemorate the 200th anniversary of the Battle. They received funding from the Town of Bladensburg and Prince George's County.

Maryland National Capital Park & Planning Commission (M-NCPPC)

M-NCPPC was a partner and supporter in planning and building the monument. The M-NCPPC Department of Parks and Recreation has administrative offices near Bladensburg.

Aman Trust representatives held periodic review meetings with M-NCPPC for updates on the monument's plans and progress. Samuel J. Parker, Jr. was the Chairman, and Edward Day was the representative on the Task Force. Others involved included Anthony Nolan, a manager, and Lynn Gulley, a landscape architect, who managed the improvements to the site.

Prince George's County

County Executive Rushern Baker and Council Member Andrea Harrison coordinated funding for local events commemorating the 200th Anniversary of the Battle of Bladensburg.

Town of Bladensburg

Bladensburg Mayor Walter James and the Town Council members funded the Battle of Bladensburg's 200th anniversary activities.

Anacostia Trails Heritage Area

Anacostia Trails Heritage Area (ATHA or Maryland Milestones) is a state-funded, non-profit organization that manages the state heritage area in Prince George's County. Aaron Marcavitch was the Executive Director.

Others

Others included Rufus Lusk, a property owner, and James Foster with the Anacostia Watershed Society.

The Acknowledgments Panel lists those who supported the monument.

Acknowledgments Panel

The Trustees of the Aman Memorial Trust are grateful to all donors, including the major participants listed below whose help and support made possible this memorial to the Battle of Bladensburg:

State of Maryland, Martin J. O'Malley, Governor * Maryland Senate, Thomas V. Mike Miller, Jr., President * Maryland House of Delegates, Michael E. Busch, Speaker * Comptroller of Maryland, Peter V.R. Franchot * Treasurer of Maryland, Nancy K. Kopp * Senator Victor R. Ramirez * Delegate Doyle L. Niemann * Delegate James E. Proctor, Jr. * Delegate Joseph f. Vallario, Jr. * Delegate Jolene Ivey * Delegate Michael G. Summers * Prince George's County, Rushern L. Baker III, County Executive * Maryland-National Capital Park and Planning Commission * Maryland Heritage Areas Authority * Anacostia Trails Heritage Area * Maryland War of 1812 Bicentennial Commission * Prince George's County Council * Council Member Andrea Harrison

Joanna Campbell Blake, Sculptor and Monument Designer

George and Carmel Aman Memorial Trust * American Legion, Post #59, Thad Dulin * Anacostia Trails Heritage Area * Anacostia Watershed Society * Bladensburg Local Development Corp. * Bladensburg Port Towns War of 1812 Task Force * Rev Eligah B. White * William F. Chesley * Community Foundation for the National Capital Region * Susanna Kyner Cristofane * Daughters of the American Revolution, Toaping Castle Chapter * Ed and Loretta Downey* Giannetti's Studio, Inc. * Mt Rainier-Brentwood Lions Club * Francis and Catherine Hamilton * Friends of the Battle of Bladensburg * John and Cindy Heller * Kiwanis Foundation of Prince George's County * Allen Krowe * Jack Long * Rufus Lusk * Ernest Maier Inc. * Russell and Wanda Maske * W.B. Maske Sheet Metal Works Inc. * Wanda Matzen * Kenneth H. Michael * Brenda Quinn *Michael Schwartz * John Sisson * Albert Small * John Sower * Albert Turner * Fred Williams * Young Men's Democratic Club of Prince George's County

Arnan Memorial Trust Monument Committee

John A. Giannetti, Sr., Chairman * Charles H. Day, Vice Chairman * W. Dickerson Charlton, Treasurer * Trustees: Lee MacLean Doolittle * John Maudlin-Jeronimo * Samuel J. Parker, Jr. * Susan Pearl * Jonathon Piska.

John Sower, Advisor, John A. Giannetti, Jr. Advisor

Monument Artistic Team

Joanna Campbell Blake, Sculptor and Monument Designer, Pagliaro Brothers Stone Co. Inc., General Contractor, Laran Bronze Inc., Bronze Factory, Coldspring, Interpretive Panel

To the Many Additional Contributors, We Extend our Deepest Gratitude

Erected August 24, 2014

Chapter Nine: The Governor's Award

In late 2014, with assistance from State Senator Victor Ramirez and Delegate Jolene Ivy, Maryland Governor Martin O'Malley gave John Giannetti, Sr. and Dick Charlton a Special Award for their years of community service in Bladensburg. It read:

State of Maryland

Proclamation

From the Governor of the State of Maryland

Tribute to Aman Memorial Trust

WHEREAS: Maryland is proud to honor the Aman Memorial Trust and recognize the commitment and selfless efforts of John Giannetti, Chair and Dick Charlton, Treasurer of the Aman Memorial Trust, for their several decades of local community preservation efforts to promote the history of Bladensburg; and

WHEREAS: Maryland is grateful for their most recent success in helping to complete the construction of the Bladensburg War of 1812 Monument. This monument stands today as a memorial to one of the region's most historic battles; and

WHEREAS: Maryland is proud to recognize the Aman Memorial Trust and commend John Giannetti and Dick Charlton for their leadership, tenacity and patriot service to the Bladensburg community and the State of Maryland.

NOW, THEREFORE, I, MARTIN O'MALLEY, GOVERNOR OF THE STATE OF MARYLAND, do hereby offer a well-deserved TRIBUTE TO AMAN MEMORIAL TRUST and honor JOHN GIANNETTI and DICK CHARLTON for exemplary service to Maryland, and commend all Marylanders to join in support of this observance.

Given: Under My Hand the Great Seal of the State of Maryland

This 7th day of January 2015

Martin O'Malley, Governor

Photo

9: (left to right): Joanna Blake, Delegate Jolene Ivey, John Giannetti, Sr., Governor Martin O'Malley, Dick Charlton, State Senate President Mike Miller, and John Sower)

9

Postscript: Personal Notes

The purpose of writing the history of the Battle of Bladensburg Monument was to:

- Document the building of the monument.
- Recognize John Giannetti, Sr. and Dick Charlton and those who assisted.
- Have the tenth anniversary be an incentive to organize documents and photos.

Why was it so compelling to volunteer to work for four years on the monument?

- An American battlefield site had been ignored and forgotten for 200 years.
- It was an opportunity to contribute to history.
- It was an economic revitalization project in a moderate-income community.
- The Aman Trust team was compatible.
- They needed a project coordinator.

I have experience writing proposals, preparing budgets, packaging financial projects, and managing business and construction contracts. I have completed hundreds of complex financing transactions but never built or financed a monument. My experience is financing economic development projects that create jobs and/or revitalize moderate-income communities.

The Monument challenge was daunting - stepping out into the unknown.

I have enjoyed volunteering in Bladensburg for over 15 years and have assisted with the Battle of Bladensburg Visitor Center, the Battle of Bladensburg Monument, and, most recently, the start of the restoration of Bostwick House.

John Sower

Bethesda, MD

August 24, 2023

Thanks to John Giannetti, Sr., Dick Charlton, Sam Parker, Susan Pearl, and Kathleen Sower for editing assistance.

Photo

10: (John Sower at the War of 1812 Battle of Bladensburg Monument.)

10

About the Author

John Sower is a finance executive and history enthusiast. He lives with his wife in Bethesda, MD. He worked as a volunteer in Bladensburg, Maryland from 2009 to 2014 to help create a monument to commemorate the 1814 Battle of Bladensburg – where Americans fought and died defending their Capital. The battlefield site had been ignored and lost to history before the Monument was built.

www.ingramcontent.com/pod-product-compliance
Lightning Source LLC
Chambersburg PA
CBHW081628100526
44590CB00021B/3644